# This city story belongs to:

..................................

Design and concept: Ira Ginzburg

Illustrations: Ira Ginzburg, Sasha Iudashkin,
Olga Levitsky, Meital Nissim-Eliav

Contributors: James Oppenheim,
Sarah Tuttle-Singer, Lotem Weinrob

Production: Kobi Shiber

ISBN 978-965-572-545-2

No part of this book may be reproduced
in any form without written permission
from the copyright owners and the publisher.

Second Edition 2018

Published by Citykat Stories

Printed in Israel

www.citykatstories.com

© 2018 Ira Ginzburg Ltd. All rights reserved.

Designed & Printed with ♥ in ISRAEL

You know you're somewhere special
as soon as you arrive – whether you
get there by car through the hills,
or on a bus packed with people,
or by train through the valley
turned to gold.

Back in the olden days, travelers
would arrive on foot. From the port
city of Jaffa to the west, or Damascus
from the north, or Hebron
and Bethlehem from the south,
they'd make their way to Jerusalem,
the place where all roads meet.

Jerusalem has no strategic value.
It has no oil, water, or gold. Yet people
from all over the world wept
for it, prayed for it, and dreamed
of it for millennia.

As soon as you get there, you see why.

We can't wait to show you our
Jerusalem because we love it so much.
All of us who have worked together
to create this project have our memories
and our stories about this special city.
We want to share them with you,
and with the whole world.

# Welcome. Bruchim haba'im. Ahlan wa sahlan.

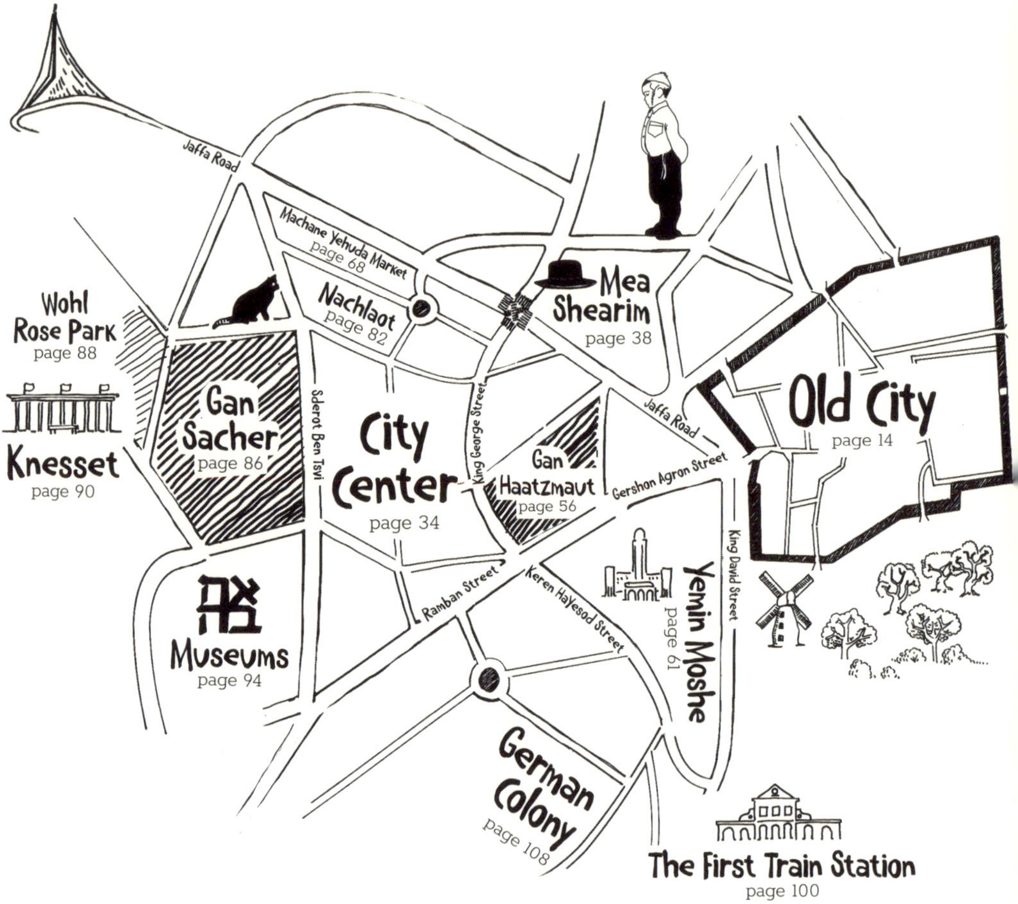

*[Map of Jerusalem showing: Wohl Rose Park page 88, Knesset page 90, Gan Sacher page 86, Museums page 94, Machane Yehuda Market page 68, Nachlaot page 82, City Center page 34, Gan Haatzmaut page 56, Mea Shearim page 38, Old City page 14, Yemin Moshe page 61, German Colony page 108, The First Train Station page 100. Streets shown: Jaffa Road, Sderot Ben Tzvi, King George Street, Ramban Street, Keren HaYesod Street, Gershon Agron Street, King David Street.]*

Jerusalem is a living, breathing city. You can't do Jerusalem in a day – you need to revisit and savor it. But the thing is, Jerusalem is dynamic. It's a circle of past, present, and future and is constantly evolving and turning. Jerusalem understands and honors its history, and looks toward the future.

Use this book more as a divining rod than a guide. Let it lead you through Jerusalem's streets and introduce you to its people.

Are you ready? Got your hat? And a jacket? Nights get cold in Jerusalem – they're chilly even in the summer. One thing all the residents of Jerusalem have in common is that at some point, if it gets cold, they'll ask you "What? Aren't you cold?" At first, it'll seem annoying and intrusive – but they're asking because they care.

Bring a bottle of water because we're going to be walking. Bring money for the light rail which runs through the city, connecting East and West.

Don't bother with an umbrella during the rainy season (December–February) – the wind will only blow it away.

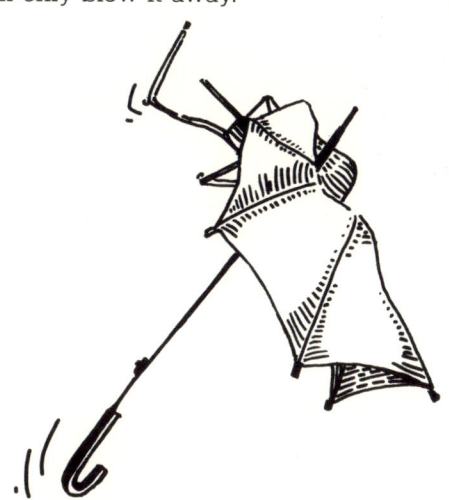

The word "shnaim" means "two" in Hebrew. But Israelis don't have patience to say "shnei shekalim" (two shekels), so they invented the term "shnekel" for the two-shekel coin.

On Saturday (Shabbat, the Jewish day of rest) everything shuts down, except for the taxis, or the buses that leave from East Jerusalem.

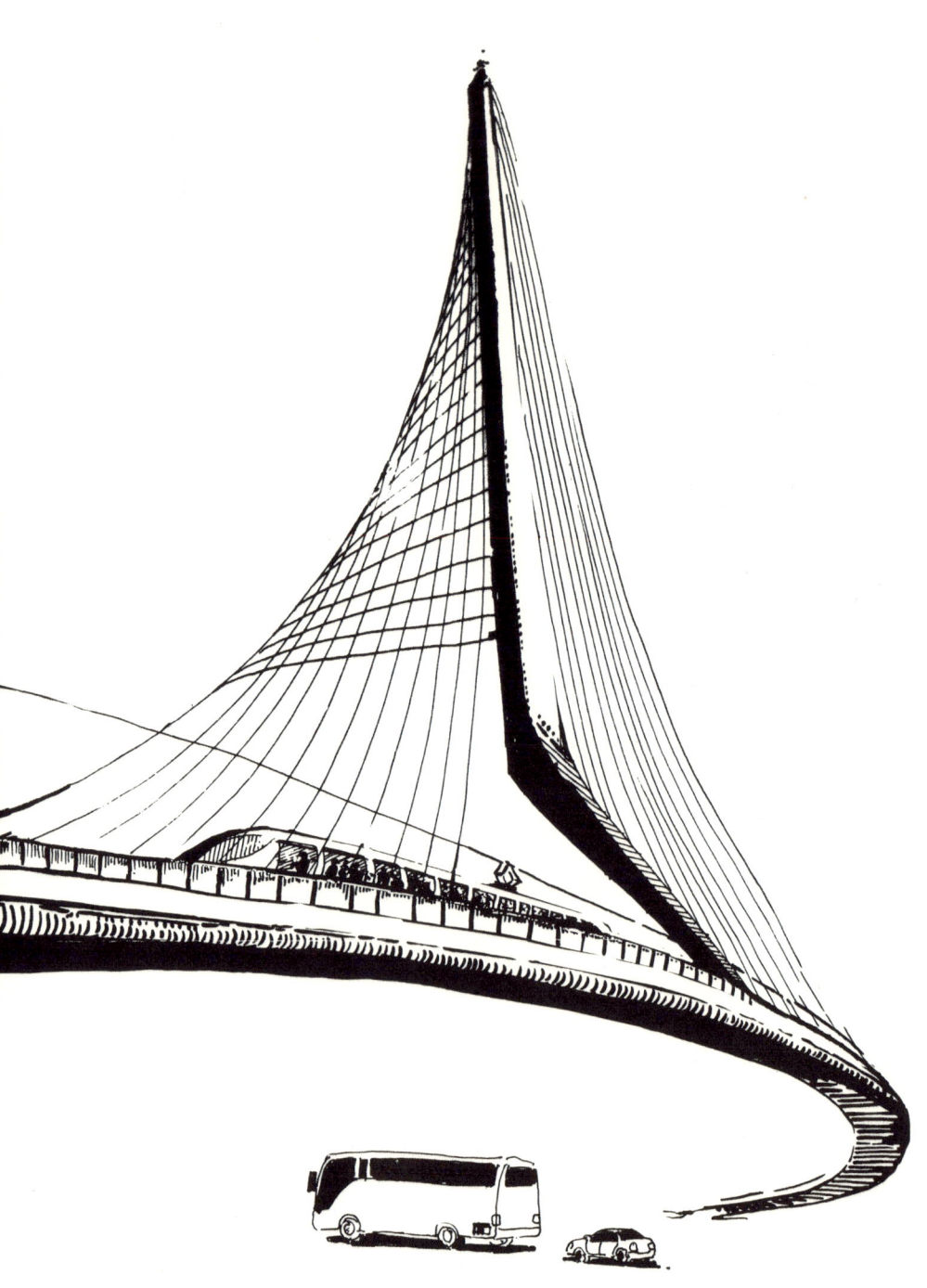

# In the beginning...

Jerusalem has no river – but it has a bridge. Do you see it? Many Jerusalemites were upset when this bridge was first built. They moaned and kvetched, saying, "It's too modern. It doesn't fit the history of this place!"

But the bridge went up – and it's been around long enough now where it's become part of the skyline, and part of Jerusalem's story.

Because Jerusalem IS a bridge between the coastal plain and the desert, the sacred and the everyday, and the ancient and the new.

# Let's take the train

Yalla.* If you ride the light rail from start to finish, you'll see many faces of Jerusalem – not all of them beautiful, but all of them real.

Tall buildings, paintings on walls, graffiti, small shops hewn from stone, mountains in the distance. Almond trees in bloom like brides in the spring. White-hot sun in summer. Big blue sky during fall. Maybe even snow in winter, falling softly against the stone.

If you want, you can buy a Rav Kav – a refillable card you use to buy several rides. Or you can buy a single ride from ticket machines near each station.

Sometimes there's a line to get on the train – but it isn't really a line, because Jerusalemites don't believe in lines. Well, that's not entirely true: There is one person in Jerusalem who believes in lines, and that is the first person standing on it. The rest may push or shove.

But stand your ground. You have places to go, things to see, and new adventures to experience!

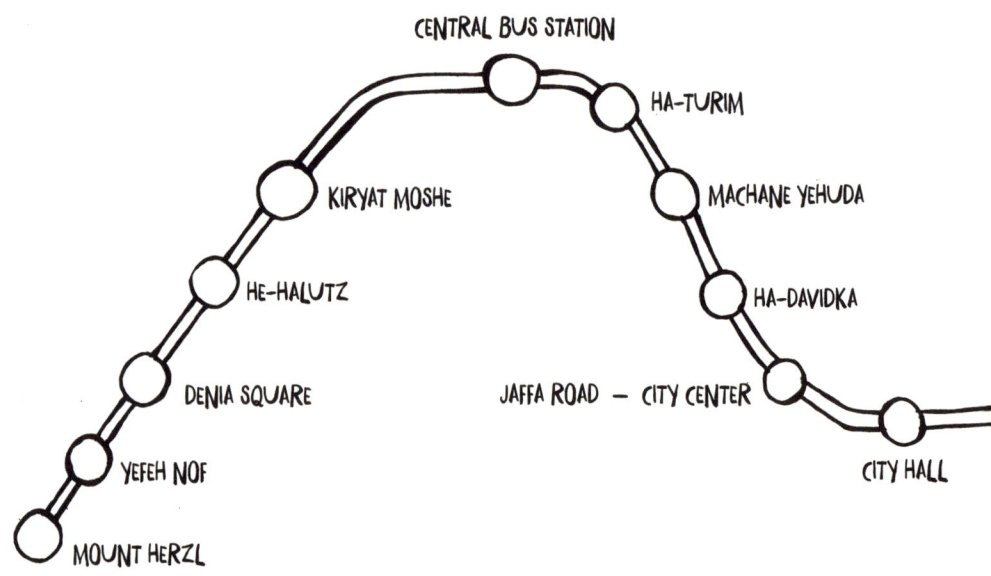

* See "Street Talk," page 12.

**PRO TIP**

Once you swipe your ticket, it stays valid for the next hour and a half and can be used on any city bus or train.

רב-קו

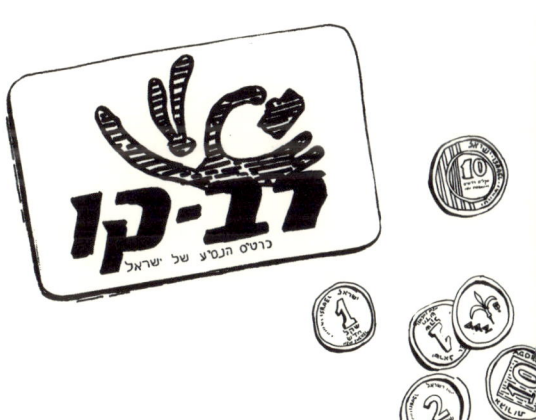

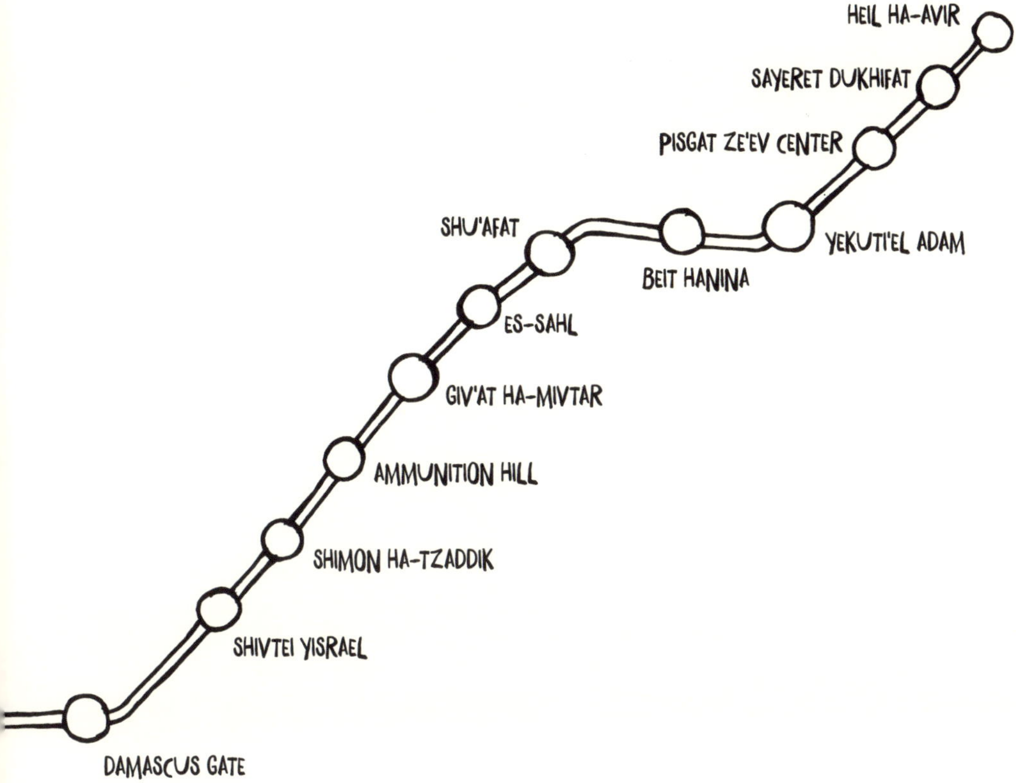
HEIL HA-AVIR
SAYERET DUKHIFAT
PISGAT ZE'EV CENTER
YEKUTI'EL ADAM
BEIT HANINA
SHU'AFAT
ES-SAHL
GIV'AT HA-MIVTAR
AMMUNITION HILL
SHIMON HA-TZADDIK
SHIVTEI YISRAEL
DAMASCUS GATE

Stop and look at all the people next to you,
and all around you. You'll see women
in hijabs and men in yarmulkes, soldiers,
and babies, and an old couples holding
hands. You'll see teenagers texting,
and a blind man with his face turned
toward the window, smiling.

What kind of people do you see? Each one
of them loves something about the city.
Go ahead and ask them, if you want.

Ever wonder what people are thinking about as they ride on the train? Write down your ideas in the thought bubbles below.

# Street talk

You'll hear a lot of Hebrew – together with Arabic, French, Russian, and English. Maybe Chinese or Eritrean. Spanish, too. Jerusalem is a city beloved by people from different faiths and backgrounds – it's a city of explorers, and pilgrims, of immigrants, and long-time residents.

| Term | Translation | Slang | Origin |
|---|---|---|---|
| Adir | Huge | Awesome | Hebrew |
| Halas | Enough | I've had it | Arabic |
| L'chaim | To life | Cheers | Hebrew |
| Sahten | Health | Well done | Arabic |
| Sababa | Longing | Excellent | Arabic |
| Yalla | Oh, God | Let's go | Arabic |
| Mastool | Bucket | Stoned | Arabic |
| Walla | Swear to God | Really?! | Arabic |
| Freier | Free | Sucker | Yiddish |
| Stam | Vague | Just kidding | Hebrew |
| Sagur | Closed | Agreed | Hebrew |
| Bassa | Despair | Bummer | Aramaic |

# Have you heard these? What do they mean?

Rega-rega

Achi

Fadicha

Mabrook

Baktana

Fashla

Kappara

Achla

Tachles

Mapsut

Al ha-panim

Dugri

# Through the gates of time

From the bustling, modern city center, down Jaffa Road, and through the other neighborhoods where people live and work and play, we're now in the Old City, a place sacred to three major religions: Judaism, Islam, and Christianity.

This is Jerusalem's heart – and you can feel something different in the air in this place that wrestles with itself on the seam between the desert and the coastal plain. The wind blows. The sun caresses.

The space isn't just what you see to the left and to the right. The Old City lives in layers – from the cisterns down below to the roofs high above where you can see the city spread before you in a mosaic of peoplehood and faith.

Each building is beautiful by itself, but from high places like the ramparts or the roof of the Austrian Hospice or King David's tower, you begin to see that the whole is so much greater than the sum of its parts.

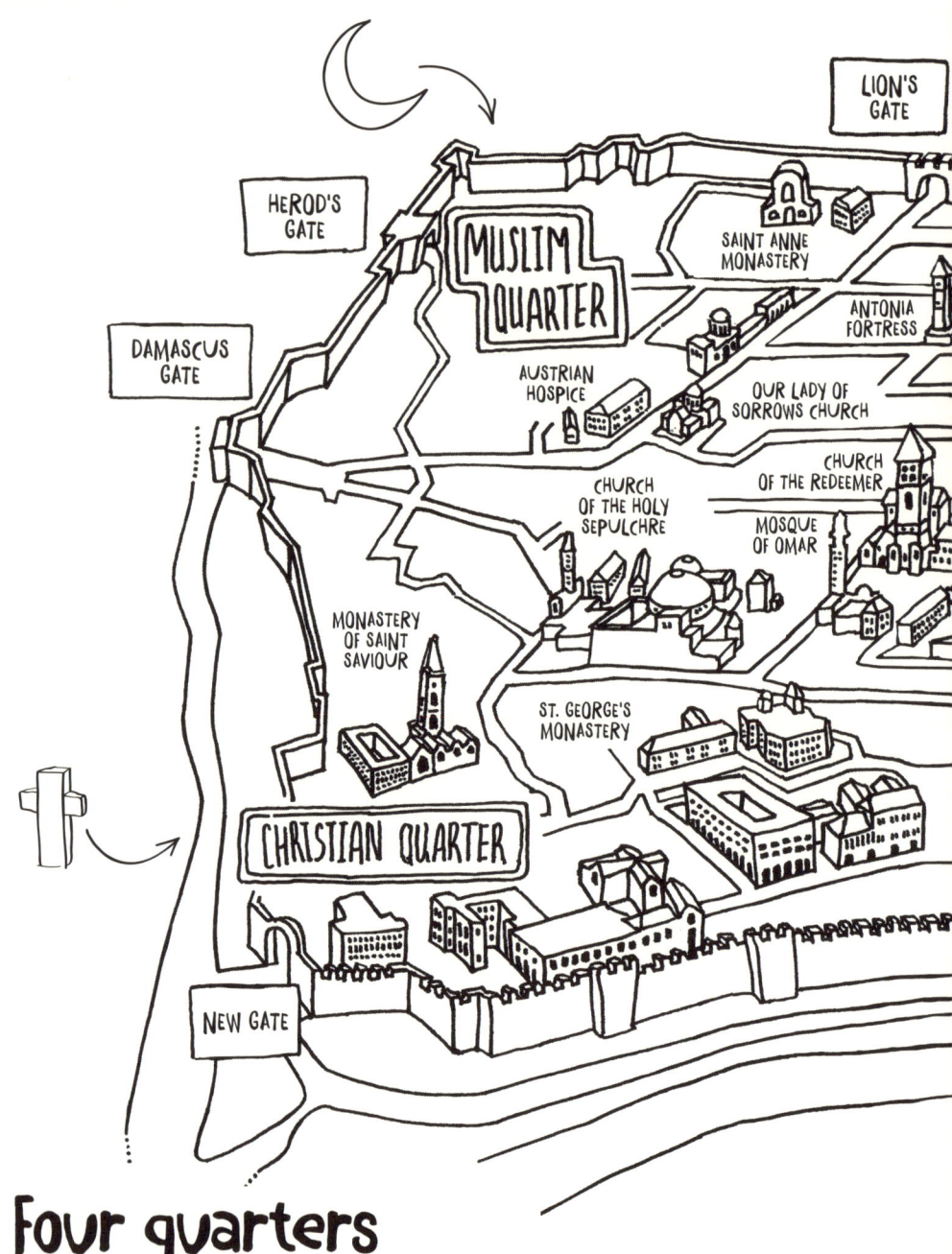

# Four quarters

The Old City is divided into four quarters: The Christian Quarter, the Muslim Quarter, the Armenian Quarter, and the Jewish Quarter. Residents from all four quarters pass each other on their way. So while you're here, feel free to wander. Explore different worlds and be part of each one.

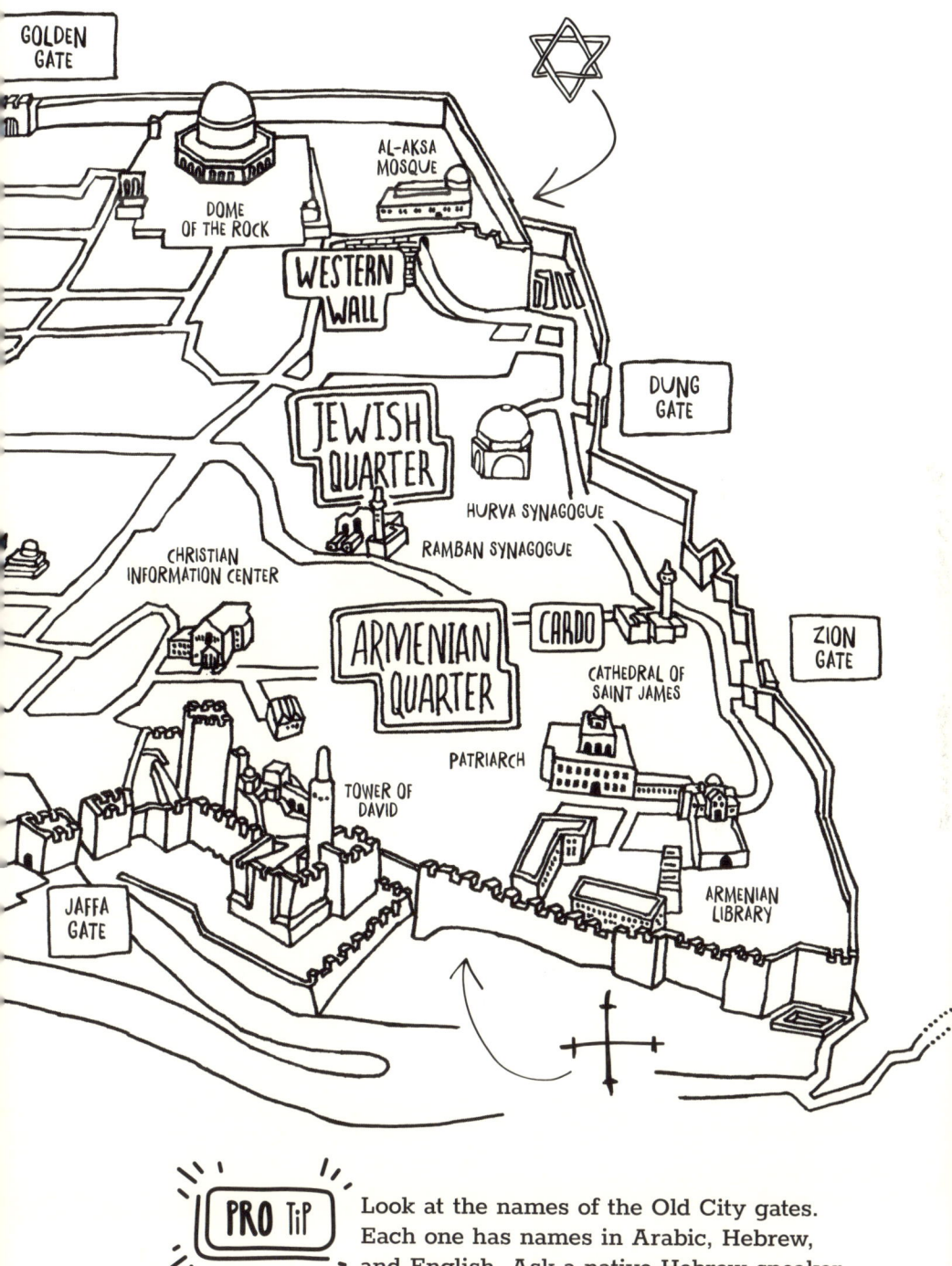

**PRO TiP** Look at the names of the Old City gates. Each one has names in Arabic, Hebrew, and English. Ask a native Hebrew speaker to translate the Hebrew name for you, and do the same with a native Arabic speaker for the Arabic names. Some of them are different – and it's worth asking why.

# Touch Jewish history

You know that line from The Little Prince –"What is essential is invisible to the eye?" It is true of the Western Wall (known in Hebrew simply as "ha-Kotel" – the Wall). You can only see a small fraction of the Wall, but it's actually huge – it runs the length of the Old City, and some of the stones are humongous.

The Western Wall is a section of the ancient retaining wall of the Temple Mount, literally thousands of years old. It isn't just about prayer and history: It's also a meeting place that galvanizes the entire community.

If you're lucky, you may see a bar or bat mitzvah celebration, a visiting head of state, a swearing-in ceremony for newly-inducted soldiers, or even a rock star. Remember: the Western Wall is living history, and you become part of that history just by being there.

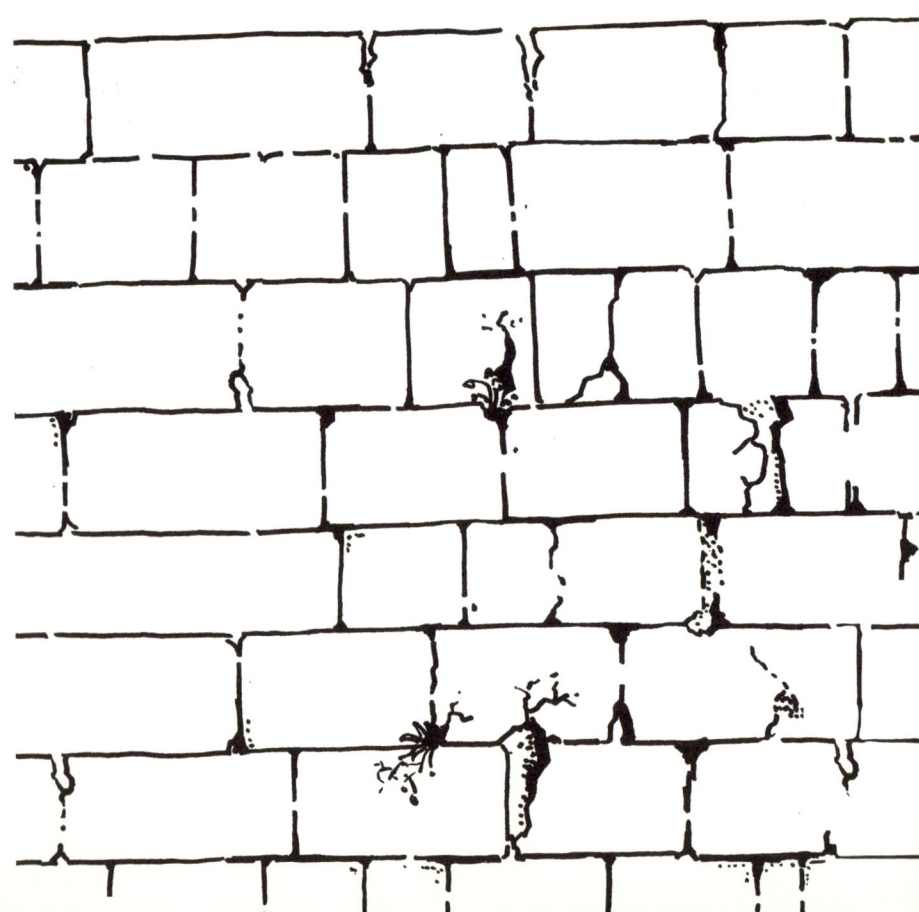

 **PRO TIP**

There is a tradition that one does not turn one's back on the Western Wall. This is why you'll see people walking backward as they leave. You can turn around once you get to Tel Aviv. :-)

Ask one of the guards by the Western Wall how to get to the Little Western Wall (HaKotel HaKatan) – it's part of the same wall – just further north. But it's usually less crowded and very quiet.

 **W.T.Fact**

The Western Wall is a symbol of the destruction of the second Jewish Temple 2000 years ago. For centuries Jews have come here to pray and, quite literally, to cry in mourning. The term "Wailing Wall" is considered derogatory, so the name "Western Wall" or "ha-Kotel" ("the Wall") is used.

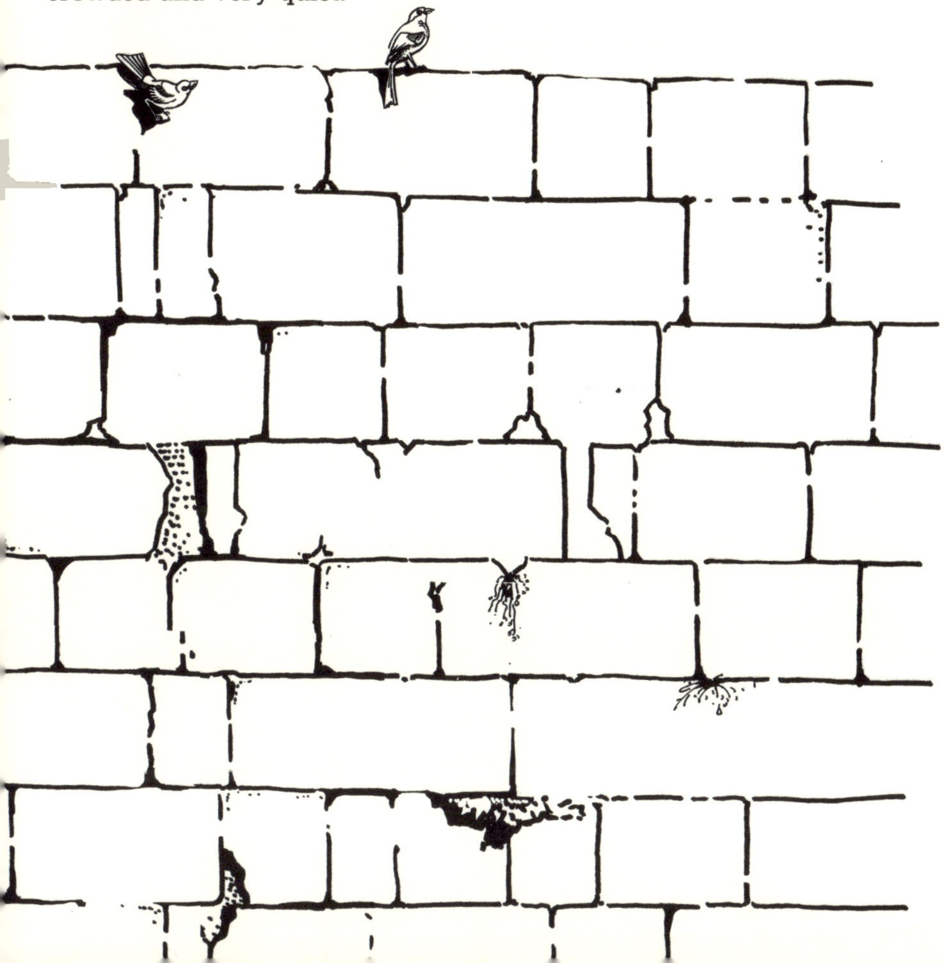

**PRO TIP**

It's a tradition to write the secret prayers of the heart on little pieces of paper, roll them up, and place them in the cracks between the stones of the Western Wall. Now it's your turn. What do you wish for?

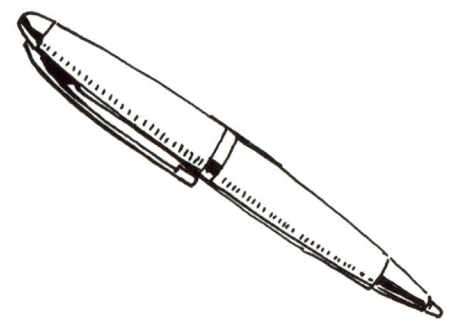

Leave a message...

Dear G-d...

Dear G-d...

Dear G-d...

Dear G-d...

# Tower of David

The Tower of David wasn't really built by King David, but the museum depicts 4,000 years of Jerusalem history, and it's worth checking out. And the view from the top of the Old City? It'll blow your mind. If you're there at sunset, face west and watch the light spread across the Old City and the new city, stretching toward the pink horizon.

# Shhh...

Here's a secret: want to hide out
in a European-style garden and drink
hot chocolate?

Then find the intersection
of Via Dolorosa and HaGai/El-Wad
Street in the heart of the Muslim
Quarter. You'll see a stone wall
with a metal gate. Ring the bell.
The door will unlock with a click.
Do you trust us? Good.

Now push the door open and walk up
the stone steps. Turn right or left –
it doesn't matter. Keep walking...
and look: Grass and palm trees,
and flowers – the gentle clinking
of glass, and the sound of birds
and Mozart wafting through the air.
You have reached a wondrous place:
The Austrian Hospice.

Built in the mid-19th century,
the Austrian Hospice was originally
a place for soldiers to convalesce.
Now it's a church, a travelers' hostel,
and a café.

**PRO TIP**

If you visit the café, you can order the best apple strudel in Jerusalem. If you're lucky, Sister Bernadette – a nun dressed all in white – will serve it to you.

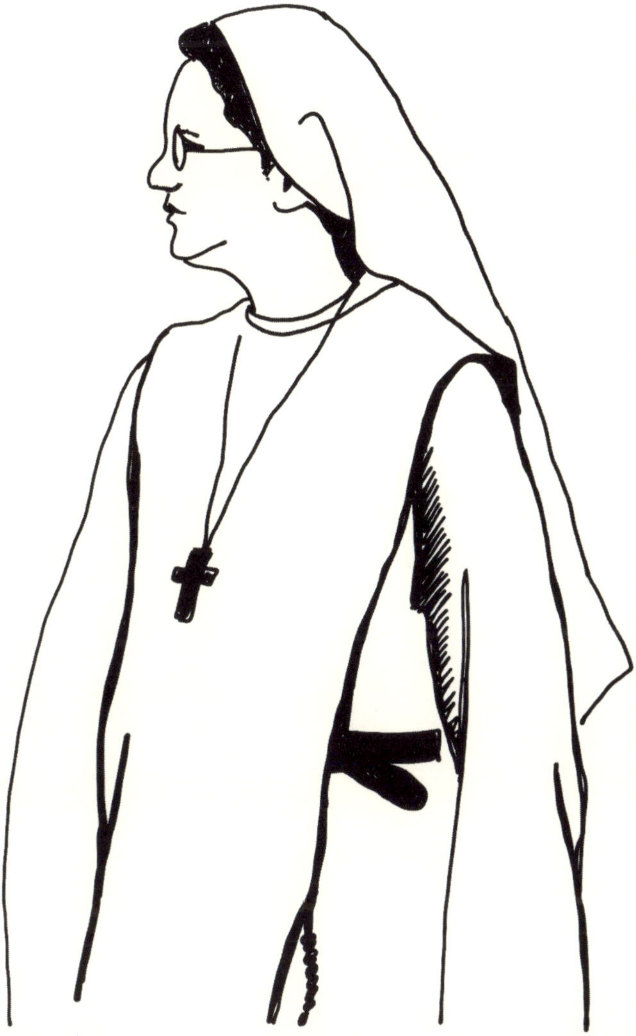

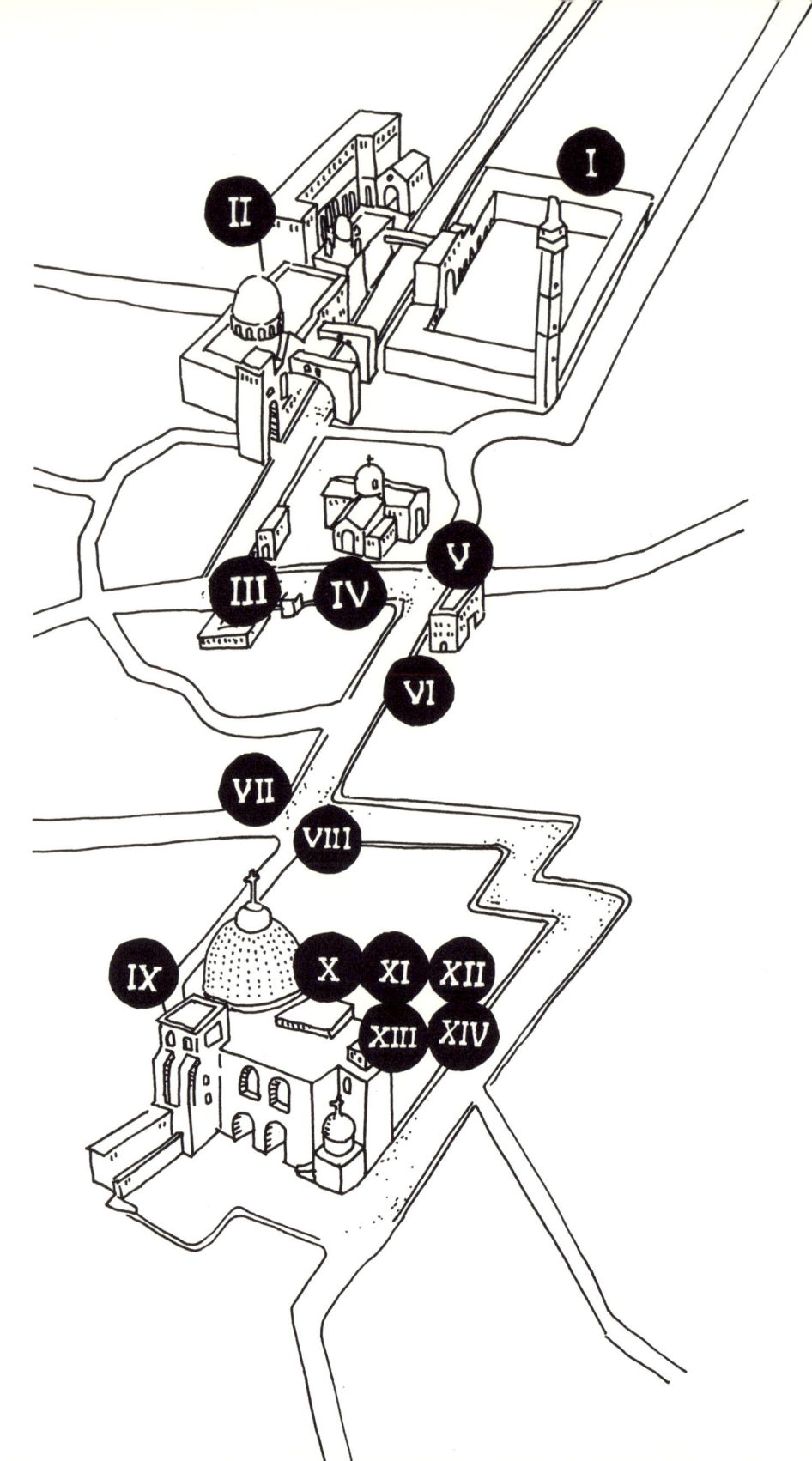

# The path he walked

According to Christian tradition, the Via Dolorosa – a road stretching from the Lion's Gate to the Church of the Holy Sepulcher – is the route that Jesus walked, carrying his cross, on the way to his crucifixion. Throughout the Holy Week, you'll see Christian pilgrims from all over the world carrying crosses, kneeling at the various stations along the road, and praying in dozens of languages – sometimes even in song, where liturgical harmonies fill the air.

**Hang out there long enough to record some of the pilgrims singing.**

# Get ready to bargain

While you're in the souk (the Arab Market), you have to negotiate. No matter what you want to buy – whether it's a t-shirt, a scarf from Bilal the fabric merchant over in Muristan Square, a ring made from Roman glass, crosses carved from olive wood, or silver Shabbat candlesticks, you must perform the following ritual:

Ask: "Kama zeh oleh?" (How much does this cost?)

If the merchant says 100 shekels, tell him 50.

He'll laugh and pretend to say no, but as you walk away, he'll call out: "OK, 80."

Then you say "60."

When he says, "Halas – 75," take it.

\* See "Street Talk," page 12.

## Wish list

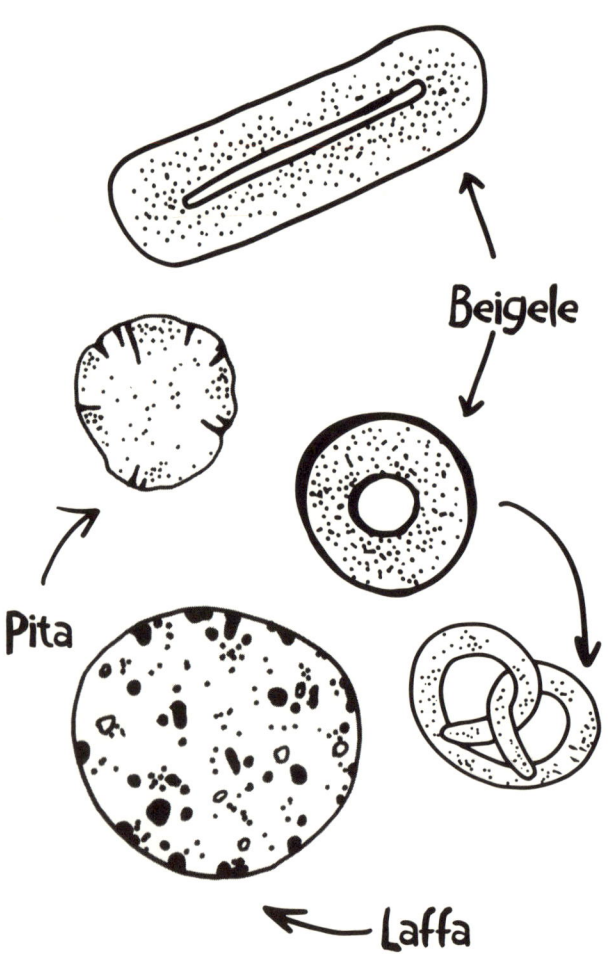

If it's early enough in the morning when
the air smells like coffee and the stones
are half naked and bathed in soft light
before all the merchants hang their scarves
and rugs and shirts and signs above their
open doors over them, remind the seller
that you are making a "siftach" – the first
sale of the day. It's good luck, and he might
just lower the price again.

Do you smell the fresh bread and the
za'atar? Buy some for a few shekels.
Take it on the go or sit on the remains
of an old stone pillar. Take a bite and savor
the fresh-baked goodness.

# Beyond the walls: where the streets have names

Take a second and look at the names of the streets you're passing. One cool thing about the city is that street names provide a living history of this place.

From Zionist thinkers to kings from King David to King George V of England to writers like Sholem Aleichem who wrote Tevye and His Daughters, to great sages and rabbis, and artists, too, the street names in Jerusalem provide an iconic map of an unfolding history.

## Streets I've walked

☐ ....................................................

☐ ....................................................

☐ ....................................................

☐ ....................................................

☐ ....................................................

☐ ....................................................

☐ ....................................................

☐ ....................................................

Do you notice how the stone façades everywhere have a similar look? That's because since the British Mandate, there's a law on the books stating that the entire city needs to be made out of this special stone taken from quarries around Jerusalem.

Why? Because the British wanted each building to reflect the beauty and the grandeur of the Old City – especially the Temple Mount.

# City center

We're in the center of Jerusalem right now. What do you see? The buildings – old and new – are all made from Jerusalem stone. In any light – dawn or sunset, grey skies or blue, and even under the pale light of the moon – the stones gleam.

# The Russian Compound

Because of its status as spiritual magnet for people all over the world, Jerusalem has always been a city of many languages and cultures. One language any visitor to the city is bound to hear on the streets, cafés, and markets is Russian. While today's Russian-speakers in Jerusalem are mostly immigrants who arrived in the early 1990s, that was not always the case.

Beginning in the mid-19th century, thousands of Russian Orthodox pilgrims descended upon Jerusalem, particularly during Easter. In order to better serve these spiritual seekers, construction was begun on the Russian Compound in 1860. The compound would eventually include hostels for the faithful, a Russian consulate, an Orthodox cathedral, a mission, and a hospital.

 The British government transformed the compound into administrative offices, a police station, and, most notoriously, the prison used to hold captured members of the Jewish underground during Israel's pre-State battle for independence. The prison building is now the Museum of the Underground Prisoners.

אנא אל תעברי בשכונתינו
בלבוש לא צנוע

TO WOMEN & GIRLS WHO PASS THROUGH OUR NEIGHBORHOOD
WE BEG YOU WITH ALL OUR HEARTS
**PLEASE DO NOT PASS**
THROUGH OUR NEIGHBORHOOD IN
**IMMODEST CLOTHES**

MODEST CLOTHES INCLUDE: CLOSED BLOUSE, WITH LONG SLEEVES.
LONG SKIRT - NO TROUSERS. NO TIGHT-FITTING CLOTHES

PLEASE DO NOT DISTURB THE SANCTITY OF OUR NEIGHBORHOOD,
AND OUR WAY OF LIFE AS JEWS COMMITTED TO G-D AND HIS TORAH.

NEIGHBORHOOD RABBIS    TORAH & WELFARE INSTITUTIONS    LOCAL RESIDENT COUNCILS

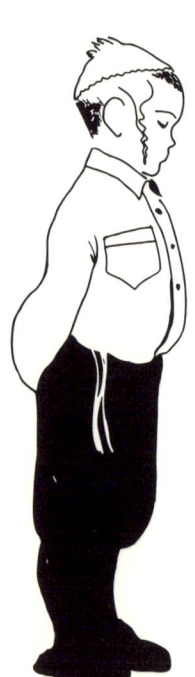

# A different time, a different place

You know what's crazy? Just steps away from the bustling city center, you can step back over a century into a place just like an Eastern European Jewish shtetl.

It's called Mea Shearim. The name literally means 100 Gates (you can count them if you want) and it's an ultra-Orthodox neighborhood in Jerusalem and it's one of the oldest Jewish neighborhoods built outside of the Old City. And little has changed.

If you close your eyes and listen, you'll hear more Yiddish than Hebrew spoken along the twisting alleyways and roads. Unlike most of Jerusalem where people can wear whatever they want, in Mea Shearim you'll need to dress modestly – long skirts or dresses for women, with covered shoulders, arms, and collarbone, and long pants and long-sleeved shirts for men.

Be sensitive when you visit – respect goes a long way. It's actually a fun and amazing place to see. A good rule of thumb: be a mensch. :-)

There's something important you should know when you explore this community: From sundown Friday evening until three stars shine in the new week's sky on Saturday night, Mea Shearim is enveloped in the stillness of Shabbat – the Jewish day of rest. There are no cabs or buses or cellphones. Instead, life is the way it was a century ago, and not to be missed.

If you want to explore Mea Shearim, but feel concerned about possibly offending anyone living there, there are special guided tours you can take with people who are willing to open a little window into their community. That way, you can ask all the questions you want from people who know this world as well as the little lines on their hands.

# Head coverings I've seen

# Coffee break!

OK. Halas* – let's take a break.

"Hafuch, bevakasha" (Cappuccino, please!) or "Cafe shahor im hel" (black coffee with cardomon).

Close your eyes and follow the scent – whether you're on Jaffa Road, or in Machane Yehuda Market, or near the German Colony, or in the heart of the Old City, or on Saladin Street, you'll find a place.

Sit down. Order up. And look around you.

* See "Street Talk," page 12.

# Which is your favorite?

- ☐ **Cappuccino kaful**
  Double cappuccino

- ☐ **Hafuch lakahat**
  Latte to take out

- ☐ **Te tzmahim**
  Herbal Tea

- ☐ **Ice Kafé**
  Iced Coffee

- ☐ **Nana**
  Spearmint

- ☐ **Espresso katzar**
  Single espresso

- ☐ **Kaful**
  Double

- ☐ **Hazak**
  Strong

- ☐ **Halash**
  Light, not so much caffeine

- ☐ **Kos mayim karim**
  Glass of cold water

- ☐ ....................................................

# Tmol Shilshom

Welcome to Tmol Shilshom, a café and study hub for Jerusalemites of all stripes.

See those big old leather chairs in the corner? They're super-comfy. Many couples have sat in those very chairs, looked into each other's eyes, and gotten engaged!

Seriously! Ask one of the waiters or waitresses if you can see the book they have with all the different love stories.

It isn't just about the love between people: Tmol Shilshom is brimming with love of Jerusalem.

Now – do you see that big old armchair under the lamp? They say that the renowned and beloved poet, Yehuda Amichai – perhaps Israel's greatest – used to sit there and write about Jerusalem:

**"Jerusalem is a port city on the shore of eternity...**

**...And the commerce and the gates and the golden domes:**

**Jerusalem is the Venice of God."**

# Hungry?

There's a whole range of places where you can eat, from a fancy sit-down meal with white linen napkins and sparkling wine, to falafel by the side of the road. Jerusalemites take food seriously, so there's no wrong choice – they're all delicious.

We know this city – and we love to eat, and we're going to tell you about all the hardcore, local places of Jerusalem that can't be found anywhere else.

Do you trust us? Good. Yalla!

## Where to eat

- ☐ Old City
- ☐ City Center
- ☐ Mamilla
- ☐ First Station
- ☐ Mahane Yehuda Market
- ☐ German Colony
- ☐ Ein Kerem
- ☐ ............................
- ☐ ............................

# Thank God it's Thursday

Sahten! L'chaim!* Want a drink? Jerusalem has some great bars, all with different vibes.

Starting around Thursday afternoon, everyone has Thursday night on their minds. The work week starts on Sunday, so Thursday night is party night in Jerusalem. Time to get down, get funky, whatever cool terms the kids are using these days...

## Beer

## Cocktails

By now, you've probably tried Goldstar and Maccabi, which are ubiquitous in Israel. But if you really love beer, you have to check out Beer Bazaar – a very cool restaurant and brewery near the entrance to the Shuk, where they brew all different kinds of beer, bitter and sweet. For many Jerusalemites, this place is as sacred as the Western Wall.

Gatsby Cocktail Bar is modeled after an old-time speakeasy during the Prohibition years in the U.S. Be sure to make a reservation, because when you walk in, you'll think you're in the wrong place – it's a little room, a bit cramped, with a desk and a bookshelf. Give your name, and if you're on the list, the bookshelf in front of you swings open, and suddenly you're in the roaring 20s... where the music is the bee's knees and the cocktails are works of art.

\* See "Street Talk," page 12.

## Whiskey

Do you like scotch? Check out Glen Whisk(e)y*. They have all the usual suspects, like Glenfiddich and Macallan... and then some more unique varieties like Ledaig and Glenfarclas.

## Wine

If you want to watch the sunset over the Old City, visit the wine bar on top of the Notre Dame Center* – they also have wine from all over the world. You'll see diplomats clinking glasses and toasting one another... and the menu is in U.S. dollars!

* Open on Shabbat

# Hamsa

Have you seen this curved symbol that looks like a hand hanging from walls or worn as a charm around someone's neck? It's called a "hamsa" ("Five") for its five fingers, and it's a symbol that's carried throughout the Jewish and Arab world to ward off bad energy or "the evil eye." Some say that if you wear one and it breaks, it's a sign that it prevented something terrible from happening to you.

The hamsa is like the Middle Eastern version of a four-leaf clover or a rabbit's foot (eww!) You'll find the five-finger design everywhere in Jerusalem, from the walls of shops in town to t-shirts and air fresheners hanging in taxicabs and buses.

Make your own hamsa

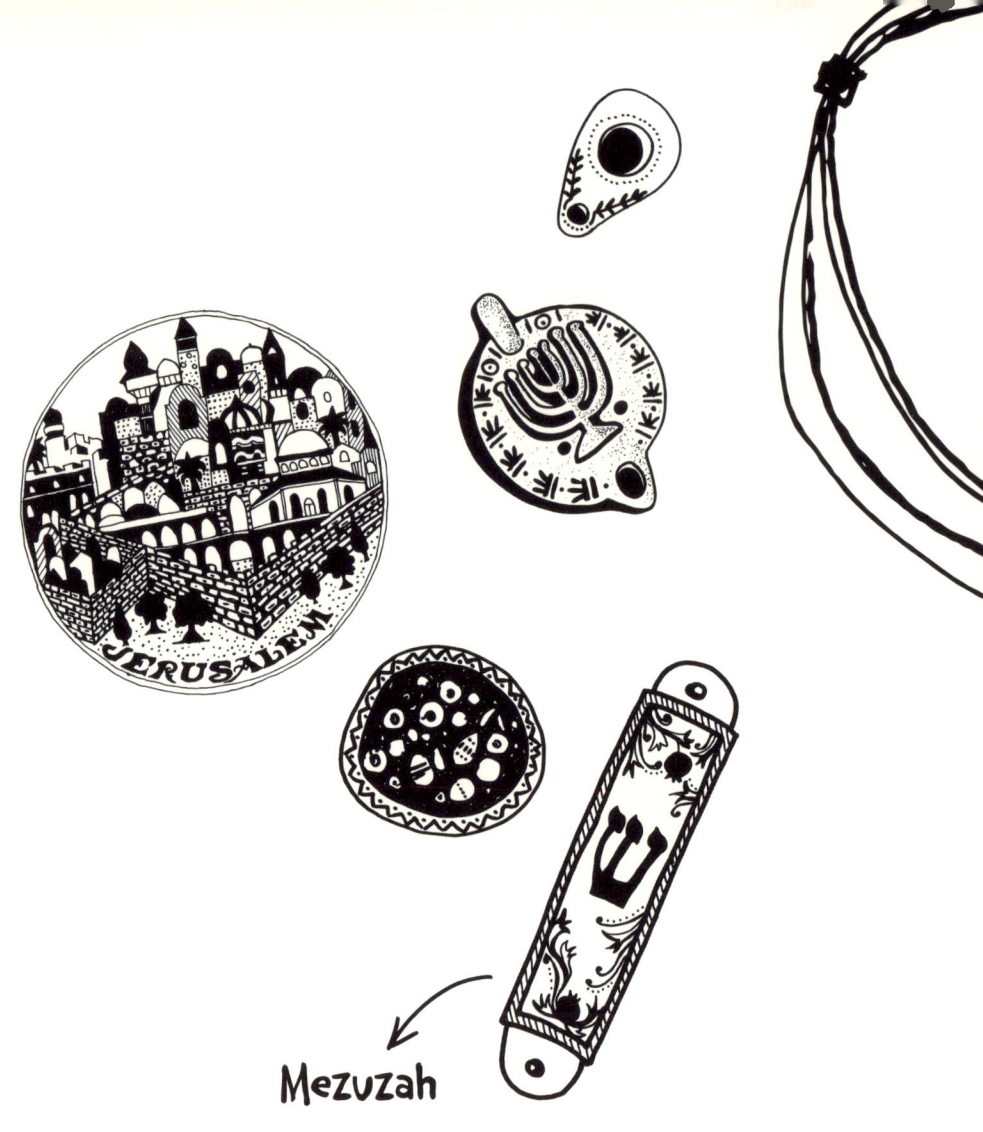
Mezuzah

Chai

# Take Jerusalem back with you

Are you looking for things to buy for your home? Did your friend ask you to pick up a mezuzah to hang on her door? Does your nana want a necklace with the Hebrew "Chai" – "Life" – on it? Does your boss want an olive wood cross? There are stores all over Jerusalem where you can pick up special things that'll keep you connected to Jerusalem long after you leave.

You can find gifts on Ben Yehuda Street or on Yoel Solomon, King George or Jaffa Road.

Over by Bezalel and Shatz Streets is a cool art fair that happens every Friday, depending on the weather. Not only is it a great place to buy funky stuff, but it is also an opportunity to meet some of Jerusalem's local artists.

But let's not think about going back home just yet – there's still so much more to see!

## My gift list

# Got your shopping list?

Cut over to Mamilla – breathe in, and you can smell the perfume and cologne from the stores. Look around you and you'll see all kinds of people strolling up and down the promenade.

There's a man with a hundred balloons just over there – if you ask, he'll twist a long balloon into an animal. There's a woman playing the violin, a hopeful lilt to the music that fills the air, along with the sounds of people talking in a dozen different languages.

If you forgot your jacket, you can buy one here. Just saying. ;-)

Back in the olden days, Mamilla was a reservoir that nourished the Old City.

Theodor Herzl slept at the Stern House when he visited Jerusalem in 1898.

After the War of Independence and before the Six Day War, Mamilla was divided and became a no-man's land of barbed wire and barricades between Israel and Jordan.

# A walk in the park

Just near the center of town is
Gan HaAtzmaut – Independence Park.
If the weather's nice, sit down for a while.
In the springtime, the whole world
here turns green, and you can smell
orange blossoms. Like dogs? You're
in luck – most Jerusalemites live in small
apartments, and dogs need to stretch
their legs.

There is no greater ice breaker than
meeting people through their pets –
and it's a lot of fun to chill in this
green space, smack in the middle
of a downtown urban center.

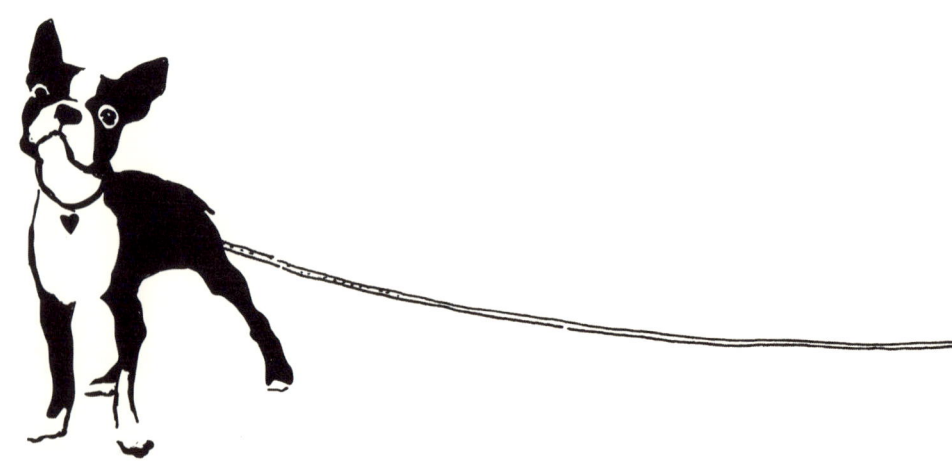

# Shabbat

There is no other city in the world where you really feel Shabbat like Jerusalem.

Signs are posted everywhere with Shabbat times. Everyone knows when Shabbat comes in because a citywide siren announces it shortly before sundown. And everyone knows when it goes out because the shops open and public transportation starts up with a sigh and a ripple.

There's a rhythm to Shabbat in Jerusalem like nowhere else on earth.

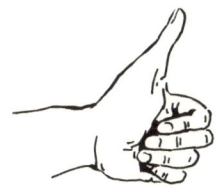

## Shabbat is perfect for

- [ ] Hanging out
- [ ] Visiting museums
- [ ] Meeting friends
- [ ] Marital relations (nudge nudge, wink wink)
- [ ] Visiting family
- [ ] People-watching

## What you do on Shabbat?

.................................................
.................................................
.................................................
.................................................

# Yemin Moshe

Yemin Moshe is a verdant neighborhood just opposite the Old City. From some angles, you can even see Jordan stretching gold and pink in the distance. The windmill was built by Moses Montefiore, and it used to mill flour – but only a few days a year when the winds were strong enough to turn the wheel.

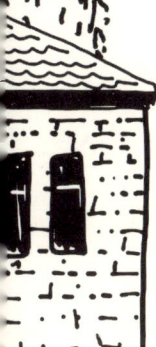

Yemin Moshe was built because the Old City was squalid and jammed with people – and they hoped this new neighborhood would reduce the overcrowding. Now it's become one of the most exclusive residential areas of the city – maybe even the whole country. #irony

This is one of the most photogenic parts of Jerusalem. In fact, it's common to see brides and grooms posing for wedding pictures in front of random homes.

# Montefiore's carriage

Sir Moses Montefiore traveled in style, and used his own custom-built carriage on his visits to Palestine. Designed by an artist named Beaufort, the carriage included the Montefiore coat of arms painted on its doors, which contained banners bearing the word "Jerusalem" in Hebrew and the motto "Think and Thank" in English.

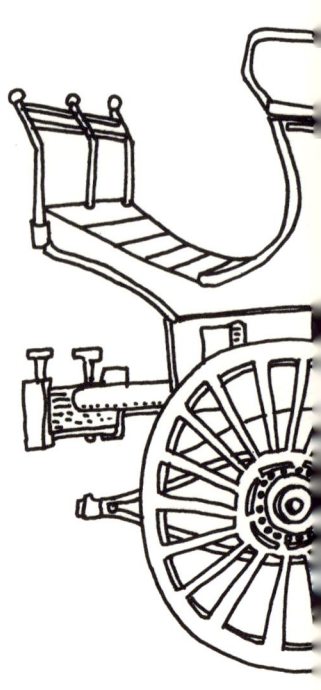

After the carriage was destroyed by fire in 1986, the Jerusalem municipality restored it and put it on permanent display next to the Montefiore Windmill.

# (It's fun to stay at) The YMCA

Over on King David Street is the YMCA. Does it look a bit familiar to you? Maybe like a landmark building in New York City? Can you guess who designed it?

It's true: The same architect who designed the Empire State Building designed Jerusalem's YMCA. Go inside and look at the ceiling. And the blue glass windows. Amazing, right? The YMCA is a little island right in the middle of the city but away from the noise of the city, and it's a beautiful place to sit for coffee, or a glass of wine, and listen to the different languages, and see all the people who come through to sit alongside you.

# The King David Hotel

The King David Hotel is one of the most iconic buildings in all of Jerusalem – the place is steeped in history, plus the structure itself exudes elegance, grace, and panache.

Like many places in Jerusalem, the King David also has a fraught history: When Israel was struggling for independence, it was the site of a deadly bombing in 1946 carried out against the British Mandatory authorities by a militant group called the Irgun.

Fast forward to today. It's the place where presidents and royalty stay on state visits, where religious Jewish couples go on "shidduch dates" to get to know each other before deciding if they're a marriageable match, where business people hold meetings, and where writers and artists sit for inspiration. It's a great place to people-watch and experience some old-world glamor.

**PRO TIP**

Enjoy a cup of tea on the terrace overlooking the Old City for an unbelievable moment of tranquility and elegance.

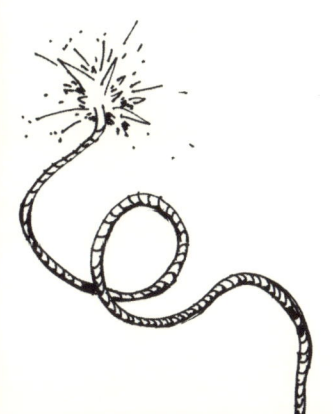

# Machane Yehuda Market

If the Old City is the heart of Jerusalem, the Machane Yehuda Market (known as "the shuk") is its stomach. So let's stop for a little while.

Buy some spices – some fresh garlic, maybe. Some dried peppers. Maybe pick up some strawberries if they're in season. Or some sweet clementines. The whole world smells like mint, saffron, and black coffee.

If you head further down, you'll find fresh almonds, raisins from Uzbekistan, and tea made from cinnamon and roses all the way from India. There are salty bourekas – small savory pastries with potato or cheese or spinach or mushrooms inside. You can also find warm babka, the sweet yeast cake with chocolate inside.

## Pick up in the shuk?

- ☐ Gourmet cheeses
- ☐ Fresh fish
- ☐ Fresh juice
- ☐ Halva
- ☐ Local delicacies
- ☐ Baked goods
- ☐ Pastries
- ☐ Spices & olives
- ☐ Ice cream

You know how you can get papaya
all year round in the supermarket
back home? Same with avocados,
or whatever you want? It doesn't work
that way in the shuk, where you can
recognize the seasons by the produce.
Fresh mangoes? Must be summer.
Figs? Early autumn. Sweet
clementines? Winter.

It's just like that song "Turn,
Turn, Turn," taken from the Book
of Ecclesiastes: "To everything there
is a season, and a time for every
purpose under heaven."

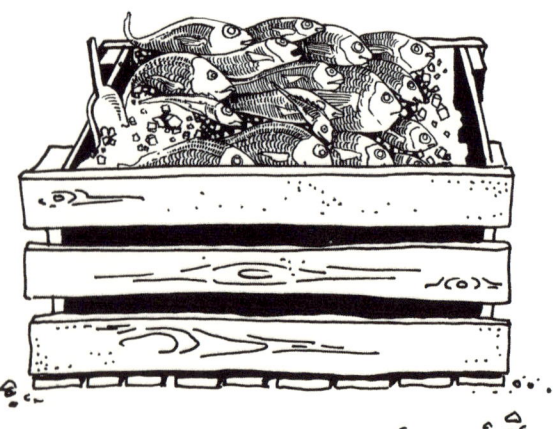

# Let's eat!

There's sooooo much to eat here,
from hummus with fava beans
and lemon, and maqluba hot
from the oven, to kibbeh made
from cracked wheat, minced onions,
and finely ground meat, to salads
prepared from the very veggies
you see in the stalls of the shuk,
to hamburgers and french fries,
to fresh falafel with tahini... and pita!
So much fresh-baked pita! And laffa –
like pita, only bigger and thinner.
And rugelach – warm, chocolatey
goodness for dessert. Your fingers
will get sticky, but it's worth it.

# What's cooking

# Falafel in a pita:
# The ultimate Israeli street food

# What do you like in your falafel?

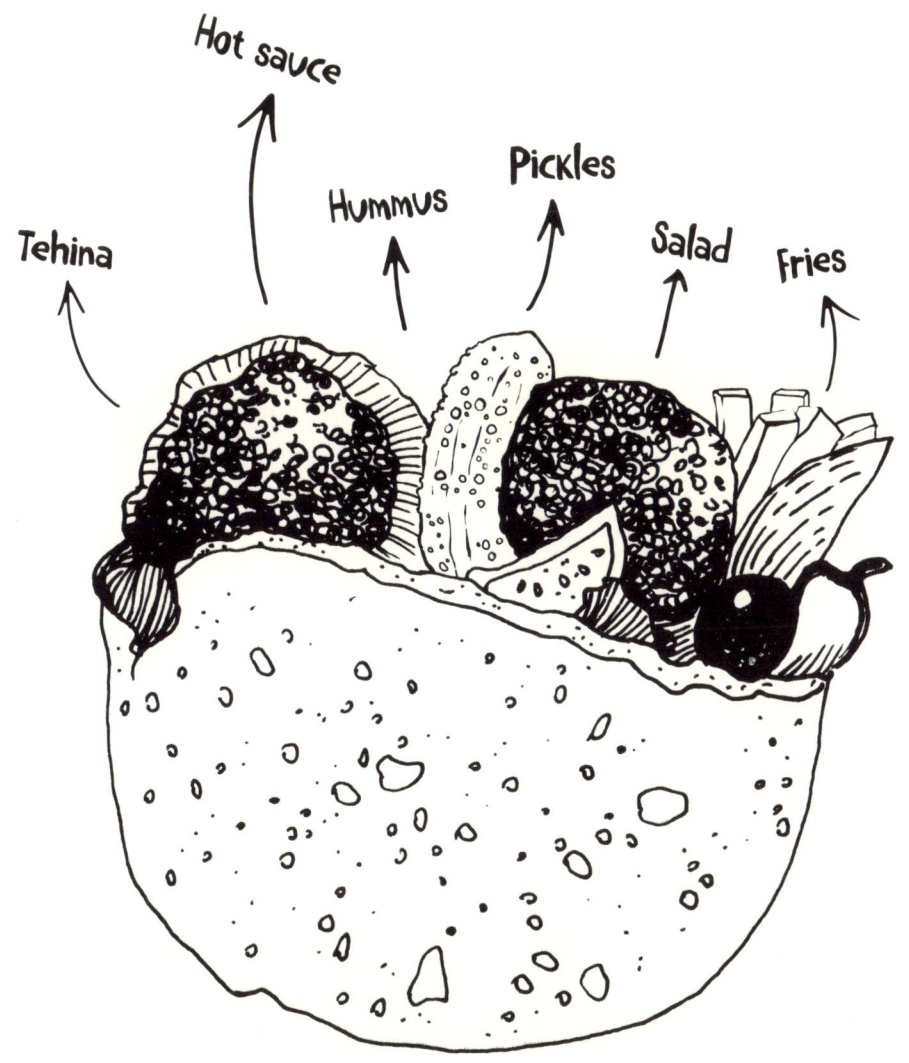

### PRO TIP

Try the slow-cooked food – they start making it at four in the morning, before the birds are awake, when the air is crisp and the sky is filled with stars. By noon, it's ready – warm and delicious.

It's sooooo goooooood.

If you come back at night when the stalls are closed and the bars are open, you'll see how the whole shuk turns into a dance party, where the air shimmers through the smoke from the hookah pipes, and all sorts of people are hanging out.

All around you are some of the best restaurants and bars, which serve gourmet food, and where you can see all the people who love and live in Jerusalem – religious, secular, Jewish, Christian, Muslim – everyone – eating and drinking and dancing on the tables.

Don't believe it? Go see for yourselves.
**#WhatRhymesWithHungry**

## My favorite places

- [ ] **Crave Gourmet Street Food**
- [ ] **Machneyuda**
- [ ] **Azura**
- [ ] ........................
- [ ] ........................
- [ ] ........................

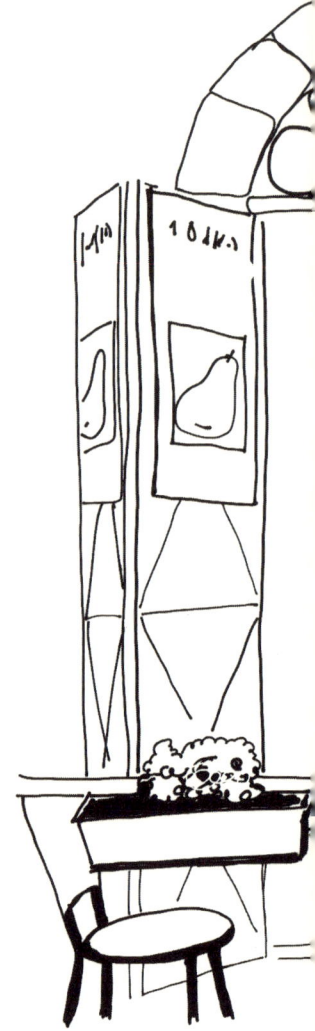

The shuk is all about the street: Street food. Street music. Street party. And street art. And at night when the stalls close, you'll see incredible art appear on the metal doors. If you're lucky, you can see stealth graffiti artist and visionary Solomon Souza in action as he paints famous faces on the doors and walls.

Walk the shuk on Shabbat when everything is closed and see who you can find. Look for Leonard Cohen, Jewish World War II paratrooper and poet Hannah Szenes, and Rabbi Abraham Joshua Heschel. How amazing is it that these famous faces are right next to the spice stalls and the fish mongers?

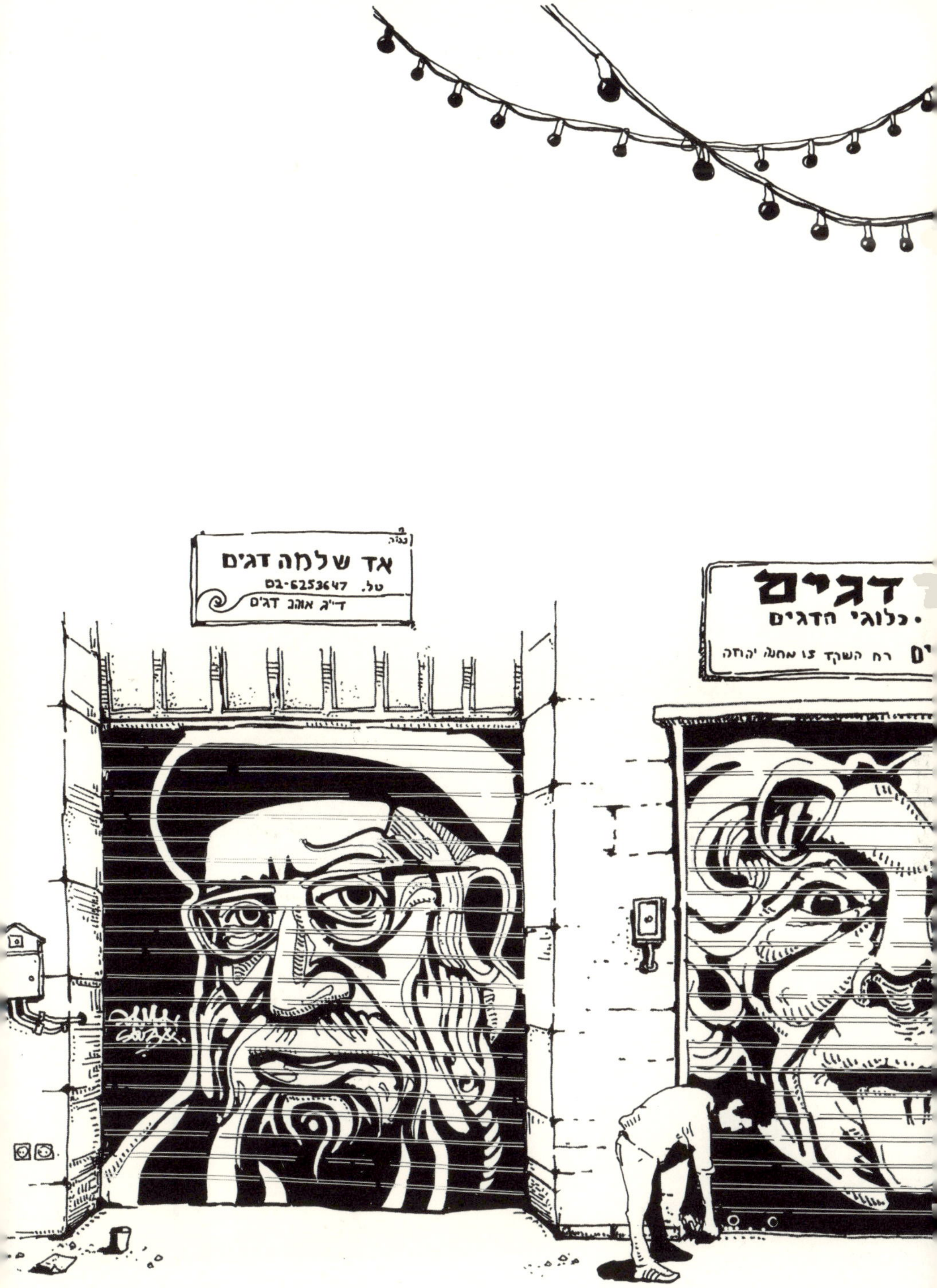
אד שלמה דגים
טל. 02-6253647
ד"ג אוהב דג'ים
דגים
• כלוגי הדגים
רח השקד צו מחנה יהודה

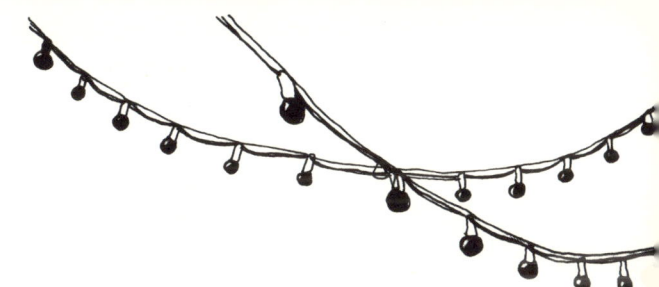

# Nachlaot

You've seen a lot – and there's more to explore. Nachlaot – where hipsters and hassids hang out, where artists paint, and writers dream, and people do acroyoga on rooftops overlooking the city. Where believers dance in religious ecstasy, and happy cats curve between the golden windows.

# The cats of Jerusalem

There's a boatload of cats in Jerusalem. Fat cats, thin cats, black cats, tabby cats, and Mrs. Katz. Cats that curl up on sunny steps, and cats that wend their way through the twisting alleys.

They act like they own the place – and they kinda do.

Apparently, there was a major rat epidemic in the 1930s, so the British sent cats to help deal with the problem.

And it came to pass that the cats took the commandment "Be fruitful and multiply" quite seriously, so while you won't see much in the way of rats and mice around Jerusalem, you're probably tripping over a cat right this moment as you read this.

## Count the cats you meet

# Gan Sacher

Where people hang out, where religious and secular kids play soccer together when the weather's good, and where folks from all over Jerusalem come to barbecue.

Especially on holidays like Independence Day when Israelis from all over the city show up and grill savory meat. You can smell it for miles around.

Gan Sacher is a microcosm. Religious and secular. Jewish and Arab. Runners, bikers, athletes, families chilling out or picnicking, teenagers flirting and texting. On special occasions the park is transformed into a concert arena, other times you can see Sri Lankans playing cricket. Basically, it's this great big fun green space right in the heart of the city.

# Wohl Rose Park

Want to see green and growing things? Do you love the scent of roses in bloom? Come to Wohl Rose Park where more than 400 varieties of roses bloom, many of them donated by other countries. The collection includes tea roses, miniature roses, old garden roses, and modern climbers. When they're in bloom in all their colors, with all their different fragrances, it's a special experience.

If you find some petals on the ground, take them home with you so you can remember.

Check out the Garden of the Nations and see which countries donated roses to Jerusalem's Rose Garden.

The best view of the Knesset is from here. Go take a picture!

Find a rose that came from your country

# The Knesset

Next to the Rose Garden
is the Knesset, Israel's parliament.

This is where lawmakers –
Arab and Jewish, native-born Israelis
and immigrants, too – from all
different backgrounds sit together
to make decisions about the country.

You can even sit in on some
of Knesset meetings that are
open to the public. You may
not understand the words, but you'll
feel the intensity. That's because
one thing is certain here: even when
leaders and officials and ordinary
people on the street disagree,
it comes from a place of true passion.

**W.T.Fact** You can take a tour and see Israel's original Declaration of Independence, along with works by Marc Chagall.

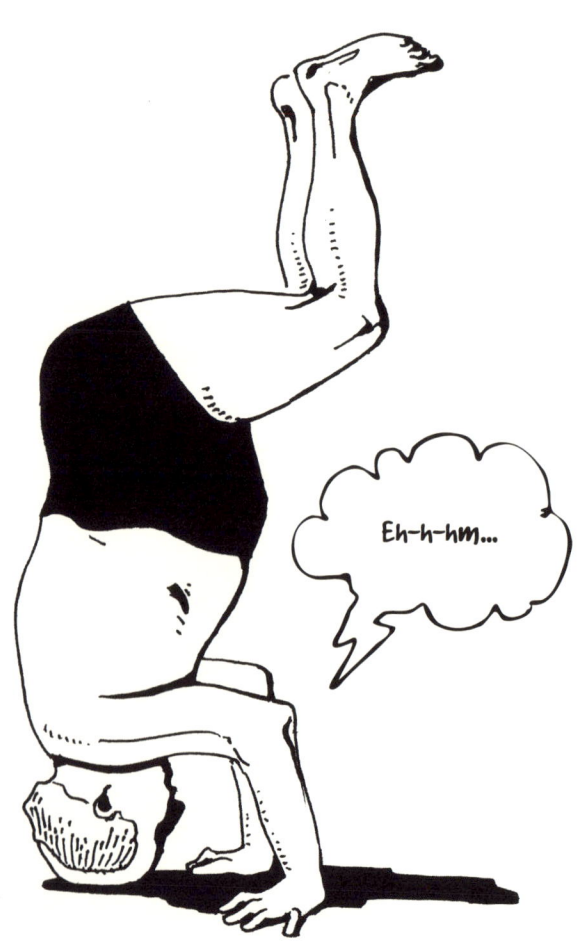

# Museums

☐ The Israel Museum offers a comprehensive look at Israeli art and history. It houses the Shrine of the Book, where you can see the Dead Sea Scrolls, and has a Youth Wing where the kids can explore.

☐ The Bible Lands Museum is a great place for families with kids who want to learn more about different cultures mentioned in the Bible.

☐ The Museum of Islamic Art houses one of the world's foremost collections of art and pottery from throughout the Islamic world.

☐ The Science Museum offers kids a great opportunity to explore, experiment, and play.

☐ The Burnt House in the Jewish Quarter is thought to have been torched when the Romans conquered Jerusalem. Today, it's a place where you can see artifacts from the Second Temple Period, and imagine what life was once like for the Jews living in Jerusalem before the Temple was destroyed.

☐ The Museum on the Seam, which sits between East and West Jerusalem, is a place that confronts and challenges visitors on controversial issues, such as human rights, through art and discussion.

Yad Vashem.

No words.

Just go.

# The Botanical Gardens

The Jerusalem Botanical Gardens
is a dreamy space for exploring.
Bring a book and sit on a bench,
or walk around and learn about
the different flowers and trees
and plants. Let's see if you can find
a carob tree, or an olive tree, or sweet
figs, or a cypress. Take a leaf rubbing
if they'll let you – and if not, take
a picture, or draw one. There's a lake
there, and you can feed the fish. Or sit
in the café, with its beautiful view.
The Botanical Gardens are a great place
to explore because they have many
hidden treasures, such as waterfalls,
a swamp, and a cherry tomato garden.

**Paste your favorite
leaf or petal here**

Jerusalem Pine

Carob

Fig

Olive

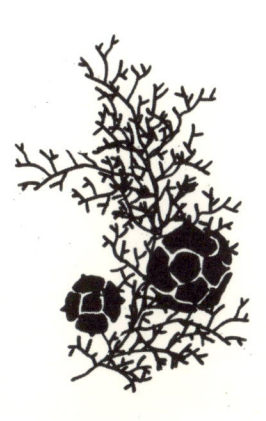
Cypress

Chestnut

# The First Station

Another place to grab a cup of coffee or a drink or a bite to eat, or to just sit and hang out – and maybe listen to live music – is the First Station, the Ottoman-era train station built in the late 19th century linking the port city of Jaffa to the holy city of Jerusalem. (Today, you can rent Segways from there for another way to see Jerusalem).

While the original train no longer runs, the First Station was restored and transformed into a cultural and culinary hub. If you want a bite to eat somewhere fancy, there are chef restaurants. There are also more affordable places, too, along with bars and cafés.

**PRO TIP**

Every Friday, there's a fair with cool stands that sell a variety of stuff, such as blown glass, jewelry, and toys for kids of all ages.

# I like to ride my bicycle

Alongside the First Station there's a bike path stretches all the way from the First Station to the Malha train station and beyond.

You can also go for a run or stroll along it, and if you're lucky you'll find a lending library right smack dab in the middle. How many places in the world have parks with libraries in them? Take a book, and bring it back when you're done. Or leave a book you no longer need. It works on the honor system.

# The Jerusalem Cinematheque

Watch a movie at the Jerusalem Cinematheque. You won't see the latest blockbuster – the Cinematheque is the hub for independent films, or documentaries, or ones that provoke discussion following.

Even if you're not in the mood to see a film, you can check out the café, which offers a stunning view of Jerusalem.

The Cinematheque hosts many Hollywood celebrities when they visit Jerusalem. Its guests have included Michael Douglas, Richard Gere, Helen Mirren, Natalie Portman. #starpower

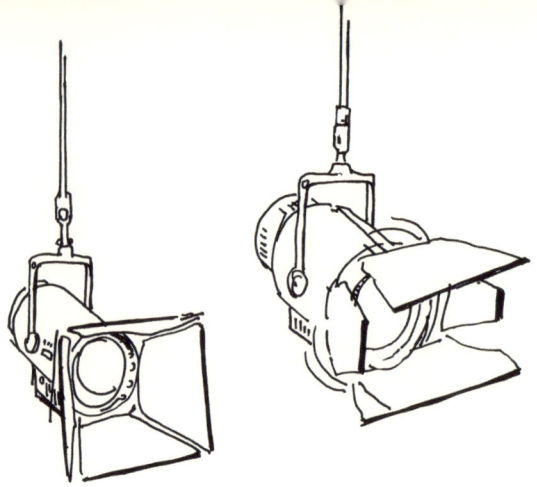

# Live music

You know what rocks about music in Jerusalem?

First of all, it's everywhere – in cafés, concert halls, parks, and on the street.

And the music is a mishmash of different sounds that reflect the different histories and stories of the artists who are create it. You'll see a band with an oud and an accordion and an electric guitar... like it's totally normal. Which it is, in Jerusalem.

- ☐ Abraham Hostel Bar
- ☐ Beit Avi Chai
- ☐ Confederation House
- ☐ Yellow Submarine
- ☐ Zappa

# Emek Refaim

Walk along Emek Refaim in the German Colony. The name literally means "Valley of Ghosts" but all around you is a vibrant community with historical buildings – many built by Templers from Germany who came to Jerusalem on a spiritual quest. While the Templers are long gone – their architecture remains. Today, the area is bustling cafés, restaurants, and shops where you can buy wine or jewelry. That's Jerusalem: a place of contradictions.

# The Jerusalem Biblical Zoo

The Jerusalem Biblical Zoo, with its panoramic views of the Jerusalem hills, is a great place to imagine the world as it might have been in biblical times. It's small enough for little legs to explore – but big enough to be interesting all ages.

Come to see the animals but stay to watch the people: The zoo attracts people from all over – you'll see mothers in hijabs chasing after their kids, and dads with black hats and sidelocks lying on the grass while their babies crawl over them. It's amazing to see the diversity in Jerusalem – and that no matter where a family is from, the kids are running the show. :-)

Since the elephants come from Thailand and have been trained in the Thai language, the zoo employs Thai speakers to care for them.

**PRO TIP**

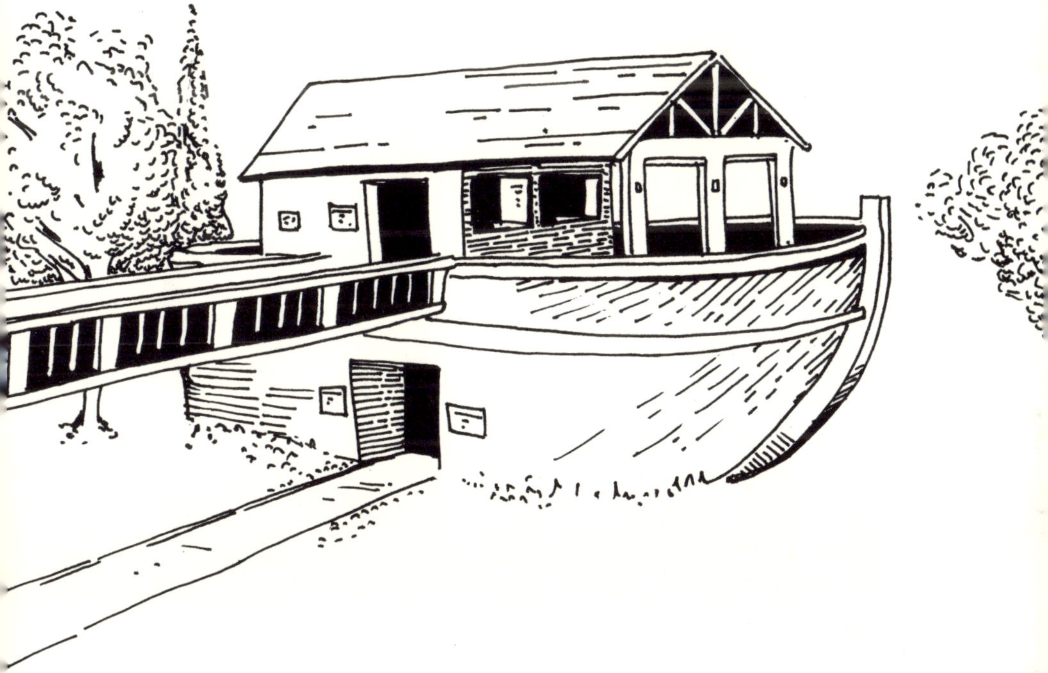

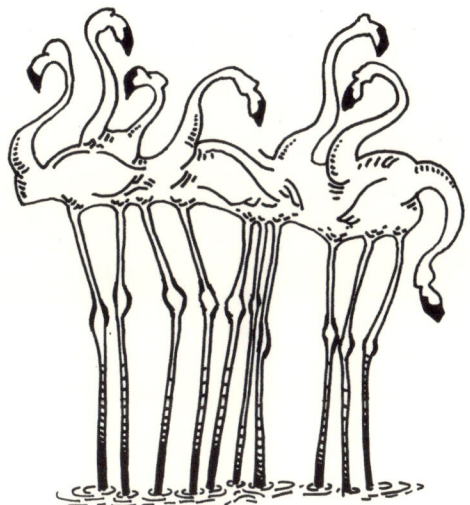

Go to the farthest reaches of the zoo and you may just discover Noah's Ark.

# Ein Kerem

Ein Kerem is an ancient village nestled in the hills of Jerusalem. According to Christian tradition, this is the place where John the Baptist was born. While you're in Ein Kerem, you'll want to see Mary's Spring, around which Ein Kerem evolved, since Christians believe that the Virgin Mary stopped here to drink from its waters. You're welcome to fill a bottle with the water and take it home with you if you want. You'll even see little kids playing in the stream – which is what exactly Jerusalem is all about: historical significance and living history.

Today, Ein Kerem is home to many churches, monasteries, art galleries, and restaurants. When the light deepens into gold at sunset, that's the best time to grab an ice cream or glass of wine.

# Offbeat adventures

Mifletzet Park ("Monster Park") is a Jerusalem landmark. Situated in Kiryat Hayovel, a neighborhood in southwestern Jerusalem, its main attraction is a cast-in-place installation known as "Ha-Mifletzet" ("the Monster") created by the artist Niki de Saint Phalle. Originally called the Golem, the installation became popularly known as the Mifletzet, and the new name stuck.

In Jewish folklore, a golem is a human-like being created from inanimate matter.

# What's your story?

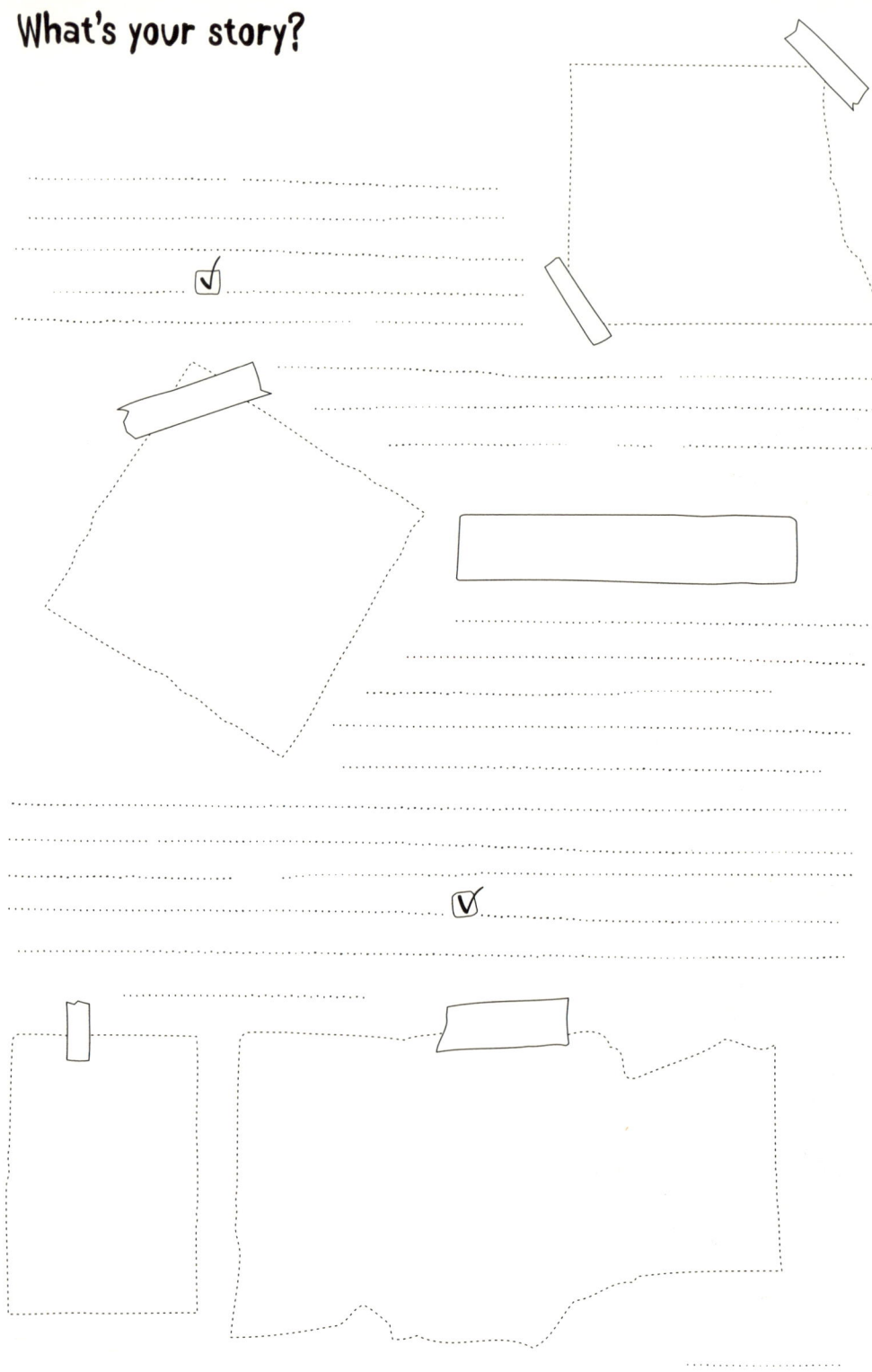

# Lehitraot!

All packed? Got your souvenirs? Got your passport?

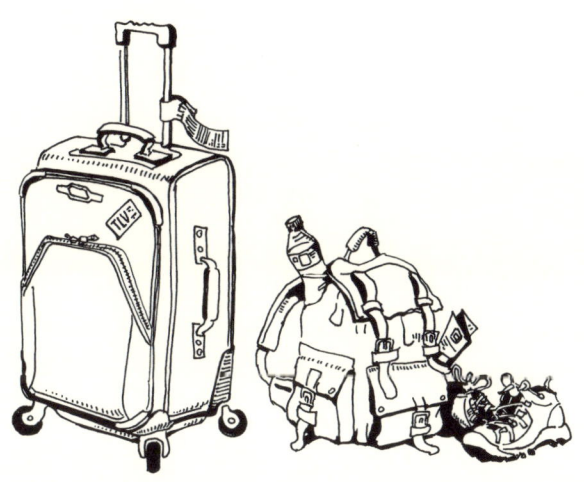

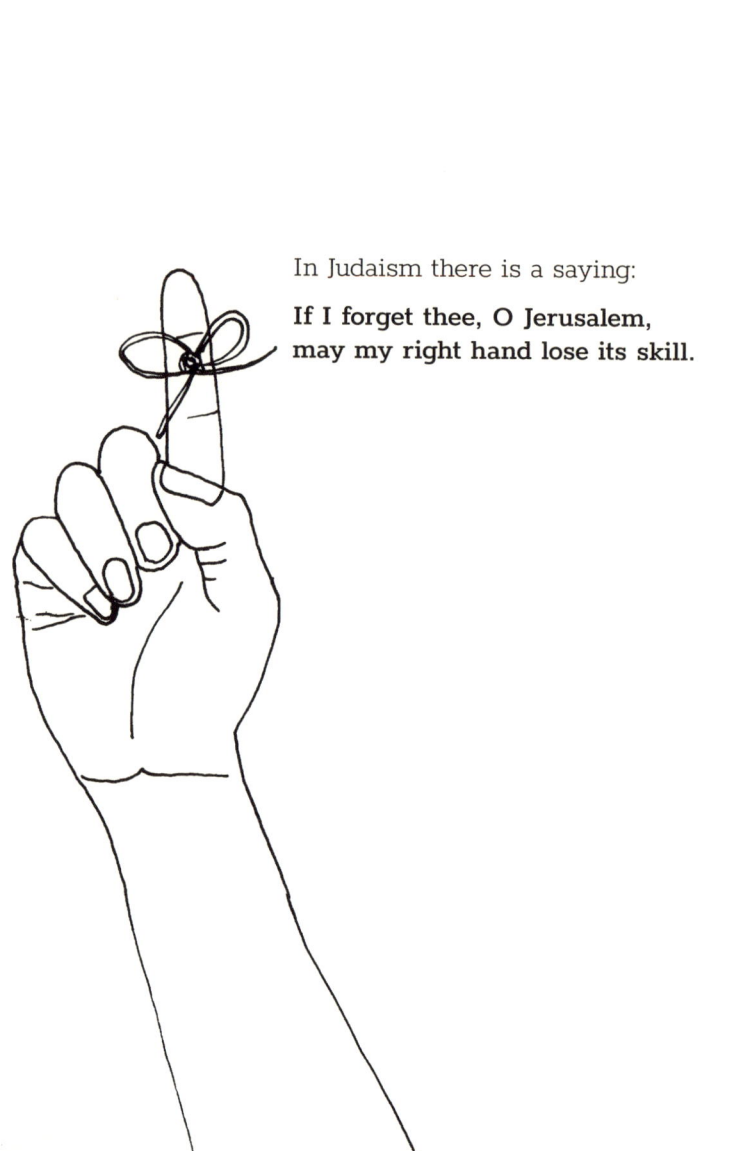

In Judaism there is a saying:

**If I forget thee, O Jerusalem, may my right hand lose its skill.**

# What will you remember about this special city?

1. ......
2. ......
3. ......

# Thank you...

..for letting us show you around our Jerusalem, our home – it's been really fun! It's been an honor to introduce you to the things that move us, and make us feel alive... that make us reel with possibilities, and that fill us with that spark of potential.

All of us who are part of this project love Jerusalem – and love Jerusalem from different angles, and different spaces. And we are so glad that we had a chance to share so many sides with you.

Special thanks to:

Sarah Tuttle-Singer, who brought her wit, light, and love into these pages;

James Oppenheim, who gave his madness and inspiration;

Sasha Iudashkin, Olga Levitsky, Meital Nissim-Eliav, and Lotem Weinrob for their creativity;

Mira Ginzburg for her late-night support;

Boris Ginzburg, who made it happen.

**Happy travels,**
**Ira Ginzburg**

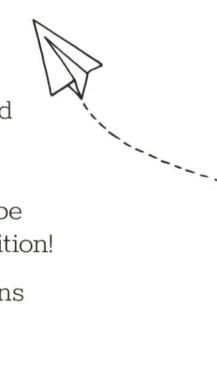

This book is always changing and growing. If you have inspiring stories, please email us at info@citykatstories.com and maybe we'll include them in the next edition!

Follow the tips & recommendations written by locals at:

**www.citykatstories.com**